make
pillows

12 Stylish Projects to Sew

C&T PUBLISHING

Text, photography, and artwork copyright © 2016 by C&T Publishing, Inc.

Publisher: Amy Marson

Creative Director: Gailen Runge

Editors: Alice Mace Nakanishi and Joanna Burgarino

Designer: April Mostek

Production Coordinator: Zinnia Heinzmann

Photography by Diane Pedersen, Christina Carty-Francis, and Nissa Brehmer, of C&T Publishing, unless otherwise noted

For further information and similar projects, see the book listed with each project.

Published by C&T Publishing, Inc., P.O. Box 1456, Lafayette, CA 94549

Printed in China

10 9 8 7 6 5 4 3 2 1

Contents

12 PILLOWS

Starflower Pillow

Corey Yoder

Fabrics: Oval Elements by Art Gallery Fabrics and Secret Garden by Sandi Henderson for Michael Miller Fabrics

I enjoy trying out new quilting techniques on small projects. For this pillow I used three different quilting techniques: one for the center of the pillow, a second for the first border, and a third for the outer border. Small projects are a great way to try something out and see if you like it.

Pieced and quilted by Corey Yoder

COREY YODER, a fourth-generation quiltmaker, has a passion for quilts and quilt design. Her patterns have been published in many magazines and several books. She owns a children's clothing and appliqué business, Little Miss Shabby. Corey lives in Millersburg, Ohio.

WEBSITE: littlemissshabby.com

This project originally appeared in *Playful Petals* by Corey Yoder, available from Stash Books.

Materials

Print Fabrics

⅛ yard for star points

⅛ yard for first border

¼ yard for second border

Solid Fabrics

¼ yard for background

⅛ yard for petals

Other

BINDING: ¼ yard fabric

BACKING: ½ yard fabric

FUSIBLE WEB: ¼ yard (based on 17″ width)

BATTING: 20″ × 20″ piece

MUSLIN: 20″ × 20″ piece for pillow sandwich

PILLOW FORM: 18″ × 18″ square

Cutting

STAR POINT FABRIC

Cut 1 strip 3½″ × width of fabric; subcut into 8 squares 3½″ × 3½″ and mark a diagonal line on the wrong side of each square.

BACKGROUND FABRIC

Cut 1 square 6½″ × 6½″.

Cut 1 strip 3½″ × remaining width of fabric; subcut into 4 rectangles 3½″ × 6½″.

Cut 1 strip 3½″ × remaining width of fabric; subcut into 4 squares 3½″ × 3½″.

FIRST BORDER FABRIC

Cut 2 strips 1½″ × width of fabric; subcut into 2 rectangles 1½″ × 12½″ and 2 rectangles 1½″ × 14½″.

SECOND BORDER FABRIC

Cut 2 strips 2½″ × width of fabric; subcut into 2 rectangles 2½″ × 14½″ and 2 rectangles 2½″ × 18½″.

BINDING FABRIC

Cut 2 strips 2¼″ × width of fabric.

BACKING FABRIC

Cut 2 rectangles 12½″ × 18½″ and continue as instructed in Envelope Pillow Back (page 5).

Petal Construction

1. Use the 2 petal patterns (page 26) to trace 4 large petals and 8 small petals onto the fusible web.

2. Cut out the petals approximately ⅛″ from the traced lines. To reduce stiffness in the finished quilt, remove the center portion of each petal. Cut through the edge of each petal to about ¼″ inside the traced line and trim away the center, leaving a ring of fusible web in the shape of the petal.

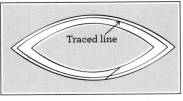

Trim away center of fusible to reduce stiffness.

3. Fuse the petals to the wrong side of the petal fabric.

4. Cut out the fabric petals, remove the paper backing, and set them aside.

Block Construction

Note: All sewing is done right sides together with a ¼″ seam allowance, unless otherwise noted.

MAKING THE STAR POINTS

1. Place a 3½″ × 3½″ print square right sides together with a 3½″ × 6½″ rectangle.

2. Sew together the pieces on the marked line. Trim away the fabric, leaving a ¼″ seam allowance. Press the seam away from the white.

Place square on rectangle. Sew and trim.

Press.

3. Repeat with another 3½″ × 3½″ print square on the other end of the rectangle.

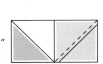

Sew and trim.

4. Repeat to make 4 units 3½″ × 6½″, 4 from each star point fabric.

Make 4.

ASSEMBLING THE BLOCK

1. Sew 2 matching 3½″ × 6½″ star point units to the sides of a 6½″ × 6½″ solid background square as shown. Press the seams away from the center.

2. Sew 3½″ × 3½″ solid background squares to the ends of the 2 remaining matching star point units. Press the seams toward the center.

3. Sew the 2 units made in Step 2 to the top and bottom of the unit made in Step 1 as shown. Press the seams away from the center.

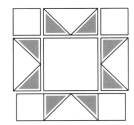

Make 20.

Adding the Appliqué

1. Fuse 4 large petals onto the corners of each block. Allow a ¼″ seam allowance around the perimeter of the block. Place the small petals in the star points and in the center of the block as indicated.

2. Finish the appliqué edges as desired. Begin and end the stitching at the center of the center petals. Stitch the outer petals individually. Begin and end the stitching at the X.

Petal placement and appliqué stitching guide

Pillow Top Assembly

1. Sew 1½" × 12½" border pieces to the sides of the 12½" × 12½" pillow center. Press the seams away from the center. Sew 1½" × 14½" border pieces to the top and bottom of the pillow center. Press the seams away from the center.

2. Sew 2½" × 14½" second border pieces to the left and right of the unit made in Step 1. Press the seams away from the center. Sew 2½" × 18½" border pieces to the top and bottom of the pillow. Press the seams away from the center.

Finishing It

1. Layer the pillow top, the batting, and the muslin.

2. Quilt as desired.

3. Layer the quilted pillow top and the 2 backing pieces. Pin into place, baste, and bind.

Envelope Pillow Back

1. Cut the 2 backing rectangles as indicated in the instructions for each pillow.

2. Hem a long side of each rectangle. For example, if the instructions say to cut 2 rectangles 12½" × 18½", hem an 18½" side on each rectangle. To hem the rectangle, place the rectangular fabric wrong side up, fold over the longer edge ¼", and press. Fold over the edge an additional ¼" and press again. Sew the edge down.

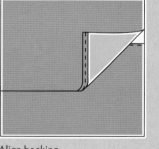

Align backing.

3. Align the backing pieces with the back of the pillow top. The backing should be right side up, with the raw edges aligned with the raw edges of the pillow top and the hemmed edges of the backing pieces overlapping in the center.

4. Pin the backing in place and machine baste approximately ⅛" from the pillow edge.

5. Bind the pillow as you would a quilt.

More Tea? Pillow

Kajsa Wikman

FINISHED SIZE: 14″ × 14″
(35.6 cm × 35.6 cm)

My inspiration for this pillow came from the vintage tablecloth I used for the teapot to give it a 1950s look. Use a blue-and-white toile de jouy print for the pot to create a different European look. This design can be varied easily through the choice of fabrics and colors. This pillow uses raw-edge fusible appliqué.

KAJSA WIKMAN is an artist, teacher, and blogger. She also runs a business, Syko Design, which specializes in happy, childlike appliqué designs and printed products. Kajsa lives in Helsinki, Finland.

WEBSITE: syko.fi

This project originally appeared in *Scandinavian Stitches* by Kajsa Wikman, available from Stash Books.

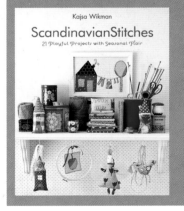

Materials

Note: A fat quarter is a quarter-yard of fabric cut 18″ × 22″ (approximately 46 cm × 56 cm).

Fabrics

NATURAL-COLORED LINEN: ³/₈ yard (35 cm) or 1 fat quarter for background

CHECKERED: ³/₈ yard (35 cm) or 1 fat quarter for pillow back

WHITE-AND-RED DOTTED: ³/₈ yard (35 cm) or 1 fat quarter for back, teacup, and plate

RED-AND-WHITE GINGHAM: ¹/₄ yard (25 cm) for tablecloth

TEAL PRINT: 10″ × 10″ (25 cm × 25 cm) for teapot

WHITE: Scrap for inside of teacup

Notions

PAPER-BACKED FUSIBLE WEB: ¹/₄ yard (25 cm)

MACHINE EMBROIDERY THREAD: Black, 30-weight

BUTTON: for teapot

BUTTON: for closure on back

EMBROIDERY FLOSS: Black, 1 skein

TRIM OR LACE for tags

PILLOW FORM: 14″ × 14″ (35.6 cm × 35.6 cm)

Cutting

LINEN: Cut 1 piece 9¹/₂″ × 14¹/₂″ (24.1 cm × 36.8 cm) for background.

CHECKERED FABRIC: Cut 1 piece 10″ × 14¹/₂″ (25.4 cm × 36.8 cm) for back.

RED-AND-WHITE DOTTED FABRIC: Cut 1 piece 10″ × 14¹/₂″ (25.4 cm × 36.8 cm) for back.

RED-AND-WHITE GINGHAM: Cut 1 piece 5¹/₂″ × 14¹/₂″ (14 cm × 36.8 cm) for tablecloth. (Buy ¹/₂ yard [50 cm], and cut it diagonally to do it my way.)

Construction

Seam allowances are ¼" unless otherwise noted.

1. Place the linen and gingham right sides together, and stitch. Press the seam toward the darker fabric.

2. Trace the appliqué patterns (page 27) onto the paper side of the fusible web. Fuse the web to the wrong side of the fabrics, and cut out the shapes.

3. Peel off the paper, and position the appliqués on the seamed fabrics. Don't place them too close to the edges of the pillow. Press them in place.

4. Thread your sewing machine with black thread. Sew with a short straight stitch around the edges of the pieces, starting with the piece placed underneath the cup.

5. Stitch the steam coming out of the teacup with 3 strands of black floss, using a running stitch. Sew a button on top of the teapot.

6. For the pillow back, make a double 1" (2.5 cm) fold to the wrong side, along one of the 14½" (36.8 cm) edges of the checkered fabric. Press. Do the same for the dotted fabric. Sew down the folds by topstitching near the edge.

7. Make a buttonhole in the center of the folded edge of the checkered piece.

8. Stitch the trim or lace tabs to the left side of the pillow (see the photo on the previous page).

9. Place the pillow front face up. Overlap the back pieces, and place them face down on top of the pillow front so that the outside edges are aligned and the piece with the buttonhole is closest to the pillow front. Stitch the pillow front to the backs, and zigzag the raw edges.

10. Turn the pillow right side out, and sew on the button. Insert the pillow form.

Stripe of Strips Pillow

Jessica Levitt

FINISHED PILLOW:
13½", 15½", or 17½" square

This is a great project for using up some of your favorite small scraps. The scraps are pieced onto a muslin foundation, and you can use solid scraps with a print background or vice versa. Plus, make it in several sizes to fit your decor. This quick and easy project makes a great gift!

Materials

PRINT: ⅝ yard (for main front and back body)

SOLID SCRAPS: enough to cover your muslin strip

MUSLIN: ¼ yard (for foundation)

PILLOW FORM: 14″, 16″, or 18″ square*

The cover is sewn ½″ smaller than the pillow form for a nice, firm pillow.

tip You can reverse the solid and print fabrics for a different look. I recommend that your scraps, whether solid or print, be analogous in color to create a distinct stripe (not too "scrappy" looking).

JESSICA LEVITT has been sewing and quilting since the age of 12. Always thirsting for some new craft, she has taught herself countless quilting techniques as well as costuming, event design, and home decor. She has also designed several lines of fabric for Windham Fabrics. Jessica lives and works in New Jersey.

WEBSITE: juicy-bits.typepad.com

This project originally appeared in *Modern Mix* by Jessica Levitt, available from Stash Books.

Cutting

Pillow size	Print	Muslin
14″ pillow	2 strips 14½″ × 5¾″ (A) 2 rectangles 14½″ × 9¾″ (B)	1 strip 14½″ × 5″
16″ pillow	2 strips 16½″ × 6½″ (A) 2 rectangles 16½″ × 11″ (B)	1 strip 16½″ × 5½″
18″ pillow	2 strips 18½″ × 7¼″ (A) 2 rectangles 18½″ × 12¼″ (B)	1 strip 18½″ × 6″

Construction

All seams are ½″ unless otherwise noted.

PIECE THE SCRAPPY STRIPE

Choose scraps that are longer than the width of your muslin strip. I used varying widths from ¾″ to 2½″. You can cut the scraps to size as you sew.

1. Lay the first scrap, right side up, on the end of the muslin strip so it hangs over 3 edges. Lay the second scrap, right side down, along the raw edge of the first scrap. It should hang over the top and bottom edges of the muslin.

Sew first 2 strips.

2. Stitch through all layers with an approximate ¼″ seam. The width of the seam is not critical. The sewn line should be straight but does not have to be perfectly perpendicular to the muslin strip. It's even great if the seam is at a different angle than the raw edges of the scraps.

3. Trim the seam allowance to approximately ¼″. Press the top scrap toward the seam.

4. Lay the next scrap, right side down, along the edge of the previous one. Stitch with a randomly angled seam. Press toward seam.

Add third strip.

5. Repeat Step 4 until the muslin strip is entirely covered.

6. Flip the strip over and baste ¼″ from the muslin edge. Trim the overhanging scraps even with the edges of the muslin strip.

Completed strip

ASSEMBLE THE PILLOW FRONT AND BACK

1. Sew a strip (A) onto the top and bottom of the muslin strip, right sides together, with a ½" seam to make the pillow front. Press the seam allowances toward the pieced strip.

2. Press under ½" along one long edge of each rectangle (B). Tuck the raw edges into the fold and press again. Topstitch ⅛" from the folded edge.

3. Lay the hemmed rectangles (B) on top of each other, right sides facing up, overlapping the hems to create a square the same size as the front (14½", 16½", or 18½"). Pin in place and baste along the sides ¼" from the edges.

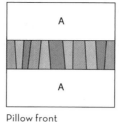

Pillow front

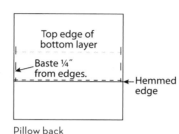

Pillow back

COMPLETE THE PILLOW

1. Pin the pillow front and back together, right sides together. Stitch around all 4 sides with a ½" seam. Trim the corners at an angle and turn right side out through the back opening.

2. Insert the pillow form through the opening in the back.

Kitten Pillow

Jill Hamor

FINISHED PILLOW:
Small, 10" diameter
Large, 14" diameter

Popular during the 1940s and 1950s, pillows of this type have reappeared throughout the decades. They are appealing to kids of all ages and are enticing propped up on a bed or nestled in a reading nook.

Materials

FABRIC: ⅓ yard for small pillow *or* ½ yard for large pillow (Cotton-linen, corduroy, or other durable fabric is recommended.)

LIGHT- TO MIDWEIGHT FUSIBLE INTERFACING: ⅔ yard for small pillow *or* 1 yard for large pillow (especially if quilting-weight cotton fabric is used)

BLACK WOOL FELT SCRAPS: for eyes

PINK WOOL FELT SCRAP: for nose

BLACK EMBROIDERY FLOSS (OR BLACK PERLE COTTON #5): for features

WHITE EMBROIDERY FLOSS: for eye highlight

PILLOW FORM: 10" *or* 14" round

FREEZER PAPER FOR TEMPLATES

Construction

Seam allowances are ¼", unless otherwise noted. Pieces are sewn right sides together, unless otherwise noted.

MAKE THE PILLOW

1. Fuse the interfacing to the back of the fabric. Enlarge and trace all pattern pieces (page 28) onto freezer paper. Press the freezer-paper templates to the fabric. Cut out the fabric pieces.

2. Turn under ½" and then turn under ½" again on the flat edge of both back pillow pieces. Press and topstitch the hems. Hand baste the 2 back pieces together at the top and bottom to form a circle—use the front pillow pattern piece as a guide. Set the back piece aside.

3. Cut the eyes from wool felt and stitch a highlight in each eye by taking a few stitches with white floss.

4. Temporarily glue or hand baste the eyes in place using the pattern template as a guide.

5. Pin the eyes to the pillow front (use the pattern template for placement) and topstitch using matching thread.

6. Repeat Steps 4 and 5 for the nose.

7. Embroider the eyebrows and mouth with black perle cotton or embroidery floss. Add 3 whiskers on each side of the face.

8. Pin 2 ear pieces together and sew, leaving the bottom edge open. Clip the corner, turn right side out, and press. Repeat for the other ear.

9. Pin the ears in place with raw edges matching (use the pattern template for placement) and then pin the front to the back and sew all the way around the pillow.

10. Notch the curves and trim seam allowances as needed.

11. Turn the pillow cover through the envelope back closure.

12. Insert the pillow form. If your pillow form has a zipper, you can open it and add extra stuffing if needed.

JILL HAMOR, a Southern California native, received degrees from both UCLA and UC Berkeley, before diving headfirst into the world of handcrafting. She was inspired to design, sew, and knit by her own kids, nieces, and nephews. Jill resides in the San Francisco Bay Area.

WEBSITE: bybido.blogspot.com

This project originally appeared in *Storybook Toys* by Jill Hamor, available from Stash Books.

Variations

Such a simple design can be transformed into so many variations. How about a dog, a pig, or a little girl's (or boy's) face? Or try a sleeping kitty, perfect to snuggle up to in the evening.

How Kids Can Help

This is truly a beginner project—one that a child who is comfortable with a sewing machine should be able to handle with minimal guidance and assistance from you (make sure you iron the back double hems). The features are the only tricky part for a child, but these can be sewn by hand if your child would like to complete the project independently (or the features can be simplified). Two circle pieces can also be sewn together, rather than making an envelope back, to make an even simpler design for kids. Leave an opening in the pillow's seam. Turn the pillow cover through the opening, insert the pillow form or use stuffing, and hand sew the opening closed.

Blooming Season Pillow

Kathy Schmitz

Fabric: Crackle Wheat from Moda

Spring is my favorite time of year! Everything is sunny and bright. When I designed this project, I wanted it to reflect my joy of spring with a nod to appliqué quilt wreaths.

KATHY SCHMITZ combines her love for drawing with her love for stitching as a designer of embroidery and quilt patterns and fabric for Moda. She lives in Portland, Oregon, and her days are filled with painting, sewing, and creating a home full of love.

WEBSITE: kathyschmitz.com

This project originally appeared in *Stitch Zakka*, compiled by Gailen Runge, available from Stash Books.

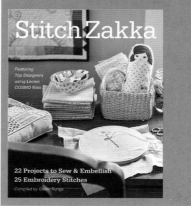

Materials

FABRIC SQUARE:
1 square 10″ × 10″ for embroidery background

BLUE STRIPED FABRIC:
4 pieces 3½″ × 7″ for pillow front (Change the orientation of the cuts as needed to get the stripes running parallel to the short sides.)

LIGHT PRINT FABRIC:
4 squares 3½″ × 3½″ for pillow front

FABRIC SQUARE:
1 square 13″ × 13″ for pillow back

EMBROIDERY FLOSS:
Variegated blue (COSMO Seasons #8025)

FIBERFILL

Construction

All embroidery uses 2 strands of floss. All seam allowances are ¼″.

EMBROIDERY

1. Transfer the embroidery design (page 29) onto the fabric, using your favorite method (such as tracing, using a soft pencil).

tip When working a design in a single colorway of variegated floss, consider how the color changes as you embroider different sections of the design.

2. Embroider the design.

- First, stem stitch all the solid lines.

- Then complete all the different types of stitches in a small area before moving on to another section.

- Add French knots for all the dots.

- Satin stitch the bees' stripes.

- Use lazy daisy stitches for the leaf details and the small bloom petals.

- Buttonhole stitch the circles in the center of the stars and the base of the petals on the small blooms.

- Use running stitches in the leaves of the large flowers.

PILLOW ASSEMBLY

1. Press the embroidered piece well and trim to 7″ × 7″, with the design centered.

2. Sew 3½″ × 7″ blue striped pieces to 2 opposite sides of the embroidered piece. Press.

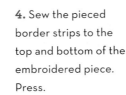

Embroidery

3. Sew a 3½″ × 3½″ light print square to each end of the remaining 3½″ × 7″ blue striped pieces. Press.

Make 2.

4. Sew the pieced border strips to the top and bottom of the embroidered piece. Press.

Completed pillow front

5. Pin the pillow front and the 13″ × 13″ backing square right sides together and sew around all 4 sides of the pillow, leaving a 3″ opening at the bottom for turning and stuffing.

6. Clip the corners and turn the pillow right side out.

7. Stuff with fiberfill.

8. Hand stitch the opening closed.

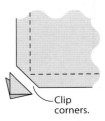

Clip corners.

Row, Row Your Boat Patchwork Cushion Cover Aneela Hoey

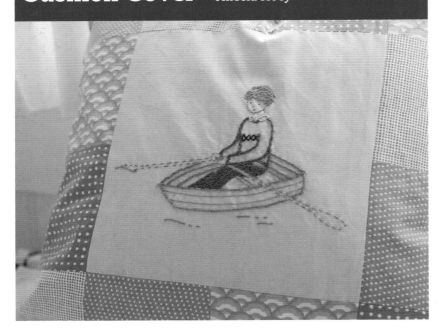

FINISHED PILLOW: 14″ × 14″ (36 cm × 36 cm)

This project features embroidery stitched on a pale, solid-colored fabric. For best results on the patchwork, choose prints that blend well with the solid fabric and the floss colors used.

Designed and made by Aneela Hoey

Materials

SOLID-COLORED COTTON FABRIC: 12″ × 12″ (30 cm × 30 cm) piece

ASSORTED PRINT FABRICS: 12 squares 4¼″ × 4¼″ (10.8 cm × 10.8 cm)

COTTON FABRIC: 16″ × 24″ (41 cm × 61 cm) piece for cushion back

PILLOW FORM: 14″ × 14″ (36 cm × 36 cm) square

EMBROIDERY HOOP: 8″ (20 cm) size

EMBROIDERY FLOSS: orange, pale yellow, gray, turquoise, beige, golden yellow, teal blue, dark brown, red, sea green

Cutting

CUSHION BACK FABRIC: Cut 2 pieces 12″ × 15½″.

Embroidery

Transfer the embroidery pattern (page 26) onto the center of the 12″ × 12″ solid-colored cotton fabric and fix it in the hoop. Refer to the embroidery guide to embroider the design.

ROW, ROW YOUR BOAT EMBROIDERY GUIDE

	Element	Color	# of strands	Stitch
Outline	Sweater	Orange	6	Split stitch
	Collar	Pale yellow	3	Backstitch
	Boat	Gray/Orange	6/1	Couching stitch
	Seat	Gray	2	Backstitch
	Oars	Turquoise	3	Running stitch
	Nose / Face / Neck / Hands	Beige	1	Backstitch
Outline and fill	Hair	Golden yellow	3	Split stitch
	Trousers	Teal blue	6	Backstitch
Embroider	Pattern on sweater	Dark brown	2	Backstitch
	Boat panels (outside)	Gray	1	Backstitch
	Boat panels (inside)	Gray	6	Backstitch
	Mooring ring (at front of boat)	Pale yellow	6	Backstitch
	Eyes	Dark brown	1	Straight stitch
	Mouth	Red	1	Straight stitch
	Waves	Sea green	2	Backstitch and running stitch

ANEELA HOEY studied printed textile design and worked at design studios in both London and New York. She designs fabric lines for Moda Fabrics, as well as her own embroidery and quilt patterns. She was a co-founder of the popular online e-zine *Fat Quarterly* and writes the blog *ComfortStitching*. Aneela lives in Berkshire, England.

WEBSITE:
comfortstitching.typepad.co.uk

This project originally appeared in *Little Stitches* by Aneela Hoey, available from Stash Books.

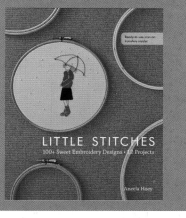

Construction

CUSHION COVER

All seams are ¼″ unless otherwise noted.

Cushion Front

1. Remove the embroidery from the hoop and press with an iron, taking care not to iron the embroidered parts.

2. Cut the embroidered fabric down to 8″ × 8″, keeping the embroidery centered.

3. Select 2 of the print fabric squares; with right sides facing, stitch them together along one edge. Repeat this step with a second pair of squares. Press the seams to one side.

4. Stitch one pair of squares to the top of the embroidered fabric and the other pair to the bottom. Press the seams toward the squares.

5. Stitch the remaining squares into 2 rows of 4 squares each. Press the seams to one side.

6. Stitch the rows to either side of the embroidered/patchwork center. Press the seams toward the squares. Press the cushion front, making sure not to iron the embroidered parts.

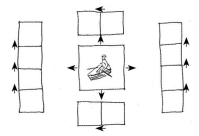

Cushion cover assembly

Assembly

1. On one of the cushion back pieces, fold over a long edge ¼" to the wrong side; press. Fold it over another ½"; press. Repeat this step with the second back piece.

2. Topstitch along the folded edges of both pieces ³⁄₈" from the outer edge.

3. Place the embroidered cushion front right side up on a flat surface. Place one of the back pieces on top, wrong side up and aligned with the top, bottom, and left edges of the cushion front. The folded edge should cover the center of the cushion front.

4. Place the second back piece on top, wrong side up, aligning it with the top, bottom, and right edges of the cushion front. The folded edge should overlap the first back piece.

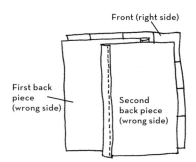

Front (right side)

First back piece (wrong side)

Second back piece (wrong side)

5. Pin and hand baste the edges together. Machine stitch all around the outside edge with a ³⁄₄" seam allowance.

6. Zigzag stitch or overlock the raw edges to finish the seam.

7. Turn right side out and press, taking care not to iron the embroidered parts. Insert the pillow form.

Hopscotch Pillow

Abbey Lane Quilts

FINISHED SIZE: 14" × 14"

Add a decorator's touch to your nursery with a pillow to match a quilt.

ABBEY LANE QUILTS was founded in 2008 by Marcea Owen and Janice Liljenquist. Marcea is an entrepreneur, writer, and designer with a background in art, crafts, and interior design. Janice is an accomplished quilting teacher and longarm quilter. Abbey Lane Quilts is in Oviedo, Florida.

WEBSITE: abbeylanequilts.com

This project originally appeared in *Baby Times* by Abbey Lane Quilts, available from Stash Books.

Materials and Cutting

Do not prewash fabrics before cutting. Trace Hopscotch Small Circle pattern (page 26) onto template plastic or heavy paper and cut it out.

Materials	For	Cutting Instructions
3/8 yard white fabric	Center square	Cut 1 square 4½″ × 4½″.
	Outer border	Cut 2 rectangles 5½″ × 6½″. Cut 2 rectangles 5½″ × 16½″.
1/8 yard black fabric	Center square	Cut 2 rectangles 1½″ × 4½″. Cut 2 rectangles 1½″ × 6½″.
Assorted scraps from 13 fabrics	Circles	Cut 13 Hopscotch Small Circles.
¼ yard fabric	Cording covering	Cut 2 strips 2″ × width of fabric.
½ yard fabric	Backing	Cut 1 square 16½″ × 16½″.
Notions: 2 yards of 9/16″ cording; 14″ pillow form; chalk or erasable marker		

Construction

PILLOW FRONT

1. Sew a black 1½″ × 4½″ rectangle to each side of the white 4½″ × 4½″ square. Sew a black 1½″ × 6½″ rectangle to the top and bottom of the unit. Press seams to the outside.

2. Glue or pin a circle to the center of the block. Sew the circle on with a raw-edge appliqué ¼″ from the edge.

3. Sew a white 5½″ × 6½″ rectangle to each side of the block. Sew a white 5½″ × 16½″ rectangle to the top and bottom of the block. Press the seams to the inside.

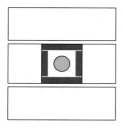

4. With chalk or an erasable marker, draw a line around the white border 2″ from the center square.

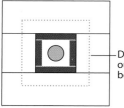

— Draw line 2″ outside inner border edge.

5. Arrange the remaining 12 circles around the square. Pin or glue into place on the drawn line. Create a raw-edge appliqué by stitching ¼″ from the raw edge of the circles.

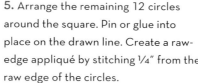

6. Wash and dry the finished top and the backing fabric. This will give the circles the frayed-edge look. After they have dried, press both pieces and square up the pillow top. Trim the pillow top and backing to 15″ × 15″.

CORDING

1. Sew the 2 cording covering strips end to end. Press the seam open and trim to 66″ long.

2. With the wrong side up, lay the cording in the center of the strip. Fold the covering over the cording so the raw edges of the fabric are even and the right side of the fabric is on the outside. Stitch as close as possible to the cording.

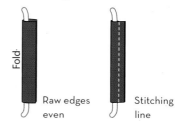

Fold

Raw edges even

Stitching line

3. Starting in the center of one side, leave a 1″ tail and start pinning the covered cording to the right side of the pillow top. As you come to each corner, make 3 small clips in the cording seam allowance to allow the cording to curve smoothly around each corner. Take care to avoid cutting through the stitching line.

4. Sew the covered cording to the pillow top, matching raw edges and stitching close to the cording. When you return to the starting point, overlap the cording and double-stitch to secure it in place. Cut both ends of the covered cording to about ½".

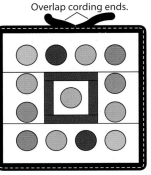

Overlap cording ends.

PILLOW ASSEMBLY

1. With right sides together, pin the pillow front to the backing fabric. Stitch the pillow together by starting approximately 1½" from a corner of one side. Sew the short seam to the corner, turn, and continue sewing and turning around 3 sides; turn the last corner and sew 1½" into the remaining side. This will leave most of the fourth side open for turning. Stitch as close to the cording as you can.

2. Turn right side out. Put the pillow form inside. Hand stitch the fourth side closed with a whipstitch.

Wee Village Town Pillow

Wendy Williams

FINISHED SIZE: 20″ × 20″

What a charming village! The background fabrics for this pillow are shot cotton in two shades of gray. Try using other colors or even small prints. Choose colors that allow the felt to contrast.

WENDY WILLIAMS began her career as a teacher of fashion, expanding to teach patchwork and quilting. She is a prolific designer of quilts, housewares, clothing, and bags. She started her pattern business, Flying Fish Kits, by selling patterns and kits online. Kathy lives near Sydney, Australia.

WEBSITE: flyingfishkits.com.au/kits

This project originally appeared in *Wild Blooms & Colorful Creatures* by Wendy Williams, available from C&T Publishing.

Materials

Yardage is based on 44″-wide fabric, unless otherwise noted.

LIGHT GRAY SHOT COTTON: ¾ yard for pillow front

DARK GRAY SHOT COTTON: 1 yard for pillow front and back

MUSLIN (OR SIMILAR): ¾ yard for backing the appliquéd pillow front

WOOL FELT: 8–10 squares 5″ × 5″ of different colors, including white

BLACK WOOL FELT: 1 square 10″ × 10″

GREEN WOOL FELT: 2 squares each 10″ × 10″ of 2 different greens

FUSIBLE BATTING: 20½″ × 20½″

ZIPPER: 18″

PERLE COTTON THREAD: size 8 in a variety of colors, including black, white, and green

PILLOW FORM: 22″ × 22″

Cutting

LIGHT GRAY

Cut 1 square 20½" × 20½".

Cut 2 pieces 20½" × 11¼".

DARK GRAY

Cut 1 piece 10¼" × 20½".

MUSLIN

Cut 1 square 20½" × 20½".

APPLIQUÉ PIECES

Photocopy the appliqué pattern (page 31) at 250%. The patterns pieces also show suggested stitching.

NOTE: All the pieces are cut from wool felt, so there is no need to leave a seam allowance on the patterns.

1. Trace the appliqué patterns onto the dull (paper) side of freezer paper and cut on the drawn lines.

2. Press the freezer-paper templates onto the wool felt.

3. Cut out all the appliqué pieces.

Construction

APPLIQUÉ

Note: *I like to stitch as much of the individual wool appliqués as I can before I apply them to the background.*

1. Stitch all the windows, roofs, and so on to the appropriate pieces.

2. Pin the tree branches over the tree and whipstitch them in place.

3. Stitch the leaves to the tree with a backstitch.

Add Shapes to Background

The curved dark gray fabric is appliquéd onto the light gray fabric.

1. To create the landscape curve, place the dark gray 10¼" × 20½" piece right side up on top of the right side of the light gray 20½" × 20½" square, keeping the lower edges even. With a chalk pencil, draw in a curved line on the dark gray piece, using the project photo as a guide.

2. Trim the curve of the dark gray piece, leaving a ¼" seam allowance. Pin and needle-turn the edge with a small running stitch close to the folded edge. Baste the outside raw edges of the gray fabrics together.

3. Using the project photo and appliqué patterns as a guide, start adding the shapes to the background. Use appliqué pins to hold the shapes in place while you stitch them to the background. Add flowers using small dots of wool and colonial knots. Make the sheep faces with little chain stitches. Add apples to the tree with small colonial knots.

4. *Optional:* Add embellishments, such as buttons and beads, for added dimension.

FINISH

1. Fuse the fusible batting to the back side of the pillow front, following the manufacturer's instructions. Press lightly, as you don't want to flatten the felt shapes.

2. Place the muslin 20½" × 20½" piece against the batting side of the front, and staystitch around the outside edges. This helps stabilize the appliqué and neaten the back of the pillow top.

3. Using your favorite sewing method, insert the zipper in the light gray 20½" × 11¼" pieces.

4. Close the zipper almost, but not quite all the way, and place the pillow frong and back right sides together. Trim the back as necessary. Sew around the pillow edge with a ¼" seam allowance, pivoting at each corner with the needle down.

5. Open the zipper and turn the pillow through to the right side. Insert the pillow form.

Fallen Leaves Throw Pillows

Shannon Brinkley

FINISHED PILLOW: 16″ × 16″

This is a fun and quick project, perfect for those who want to try out the style but maybe don't want to start with a whole quilt. This project makes both pillows.

SHANNON BRINKLEY is a self-taught quilter and designer of modern quilt patterns. She holds two teaching certifications and loves encouraging others to learn and try new things. Shannon lives in Austin, Texas.

WEBSITE: thebottletree.net

This project originally appeared in *Scrappy Bits Appliqué* by Shannon Brinkley, available from Stash Books.

Materials

Makes 2 pillows.

BACKGROUND: 1 yard

BACK OF PILLOWS: 1 yard

BACKING (WILL BE ON THE INSIDE OF THE PILLOWS): 1³⁄₈ yards

VARIOUS TEAL AND GREEN FABRICS: ½ yard total

VARIOUS ORANGE AND YELLOW FABRICS: ½ yard total

FUSIBLE WEB: 2 yards

LIGHTWEIGHT, NONFUSIBLE INTERFACING: ½ yard

THREAD: clear polyester, white, blue, orange

ZIPPERS: 2, 16″ long

PILLOW FORMS: 2, 16″ × 16″

Cutting

For the pillows, you will have 4 panels: a front and a back for each of the 2 pillows. Rather than basting and quilting 4 different panels (which you can certainly do, if you prefer), I like to piece them all together so I only have to baste and quilt once.

BACKGROUND:
Cut 1 piece 18″ × 36″.

BACK OF PILLOWS:
Cut 1 piece 18″ × 36″.

INTERFACING:
Cut 2 pieces 18″ × 18″.

Construction

PREPARE THE PILLOW TOP

1. Piece the background with the back-of-pillows fabric lengthwise (along the 36″ side).

2. Draw a line with a marking tool down the center of the piece, perpendicular to the seam.

PREPARE THE COLLAGE FABRIC

1. Apply fusible web to the back of the orange, yellow, teal, and green fabric.

2. After the web is applied, remove the paper and cut the fabric, making quick cuts with your rotary cutter.

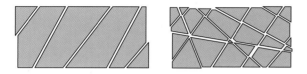

MAKE THE PILLOWS

1. Photocopy the 2 leaf patterns (pages 30 and 31) at 250% and tape them to your table.

2. Place the interfacing on top of the patterns and tape it in place.

3. Using chalk (or another marking tool), trace the leaves onto the interfacing.

4. Remove the tape and pattern, and place the interfacing on an ironing board or protected table. Begin collaging the fabric. Do not worry if fabric goes outside the lines; you will cut out the leaves. Press the collage as you complete each section.

5. Topstitch the leaves using clear thread.

6. Flip the interfacing over and cut out the leaves on the drawn line. Do not worry if you cut some stitches; all loose stitches will be caught when the leaves are appliquéd onto the background.

7. Place each leaf in the center of its panel. Be sure each leaf is completely flat and smoothed out, and then pin it in place.

8. Embroider around all the edges of the leaves, using a satin stitch with thread that matches each leaf.

NOTE: I quilted the veins inside the leaves and whimsical swirls on the background to imply wind.

Quilt

1. Baste the backing, batting, and pieced pillow fronts and backs.

2. Quilt as desired.

3. Cut along the seam between the leaves and the back of the pillow fabric, as well as along the line drawn down the center. You should have 4 equal panels. Trim each to a 16½" square with the leaves centered.

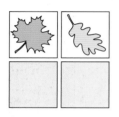

Install the Zipper

1. Place the right side of the zipper on the bottom edge of the right side of a leaf panel, and pin in place.

2. Using a zipper foot, sew the zipper to the panel with about a ¼" seam allowance.

3. Line up the leaf panel with the back of the pillow, right sides together. Pin the right side of the zipper to the right side of the bottom edge of the pillow back. Sew the zipper to that panel.

4. Press the seams away from the zipper.

Put Together the Pillow

1. With right sides facing, line up the 2 panels and pin in place. Unzip the zipper about halfway.

2. Sew around the 3 pinned sides with a ¼" seam allowance. Trim the corners.

3. Unzip the zipper completely and turn the pillow cover right side out. Press the finished pillow cover.

4. Repeat for the other pillow.

5. Insert the pillow forms, gently filling the corners, and zip the covers closed.

Breeze Pillow

Sherri McConnell

FINISHED BLOCK: 12" × 12"

FINISHED PILLOW: 16" × 16"

Fabrics: Lucy's Crab Shack by Sweetwater for Moda

With the straight edges and rounded outside, this Dresden block is classic and modern, too. Nine of these blocks separated by patchwork sashing would make a stunning wall hanging!

Pieced and hand quilted by Sherri McConnell

Materials

ASSORTED PRINTS: 1 charm pack (5″ × 5″ squares) or ¾ yard total

WHITE SOLID: ½ yard

MUSLIN: ½ yard

PILLOW BACK: ⅝ yard

BINDING: ¼ yard

BATTING: 18″ × 18″

PILLOW FORM: 16″ × 16″ square

FREEZER PAPER: for making templates

OTHER NOTIONS:

Spray starch

Small, inexpensive paintbrush

Cutting

Make your own templates, using the patterns (page 32), or use a purchased template.

ASSORTED PRINTS

Cut 20 Dresden blades.

Cut 1 center circle ¼″–⅜″ larger than template on all sides.

Cut 28 squares 2½″ × 2½″ for pillow border.

WHITE SOLID: Cut 1 square 15″ × 15″.

MUSLIN: Cut 1 square 18″ × 18″.

PILLOW BACK FABRIC: Cut 1 square 16½″ × 16½″ and 1 rectangle 14″ × 16½″.

BINDING: Cut 2 strips 2¼″ × width of fabric.

SHERRI McCONNELL, inspired by a rich family heritage of women who love sewing, began to sew at age 10. In the early 1990s, encouraged and taught by her grandmother, she began her quilting journey. Through blogging and creating, she has come to love designing and sharing her quilting. She lives in rural southern Nevada.

WEBSITE: aquiltinglife.com

This project originally appeared in *Fresh Family Traditions* by Sherri McConnell, available from C&T Publishing.

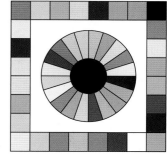

Construction

BLOCK ASSEMBLY

Seam allowances are ¼″ unless otherwise noted.

1. Sew the Dresden blades together in pairs. Press to one side. Sew the blade pairs together into a circle. Take extra care when sewing and pressing so that you don't stretch the bias edges.

Sew blades together.

2. Spray a little of the spray starch into a small cup. With the paintbrush, paint the edges of the center circle with spray starch.

3. Using the tip of your iron or a small craft iron, press the edges of the circle over the freezer-paper template.

4. When cool, remove the template and press the circle again.

5. Appliqué the center circle to the center of the Dresden circle using your favorite method.

6. Make a freezer-paper template as you did for the Dresden blade using the outer circle pattern (page 32). The circle should be 9¾″ diameter.

7. Center the large freezer-paper circle template on the wrong side of the Dresden circle. Press. Press the edges of the circle over the edges of freezer-paper template using the paintbrush and spray starch.

8. Center the Dresden on the background and appliqué it in place.

9. Trim the background square with the Dresden appliqué to 12½″ × 12½″.

10. Sew together the 2½″ × 2½″ squares into 2 strips of 6 squares each and 2 strips of 8 squares each. Press seam allowances in one direction.

Make 2 of each.

11. Sew the 6-square strips to the left and right sides of the pillow top. Press toward the pillow.

12. Sew the 8-square strips to the top and bottom of the pillow top. Press toward the pillow.

13. Staystitch around all the edges of the pillow top using a ⅛″ seam.

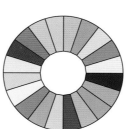

Pillow top assembly

PILLOW ASSEMBLY

1. Place the batting on the muslin. Center the pillow top right side up on the batting and hand or machine quilt as desired.

2. Trim the batting and muslin even with the edges of the pillow top.

3. Make the pillow back by folding in and pressing ¼″ on one 16½″ edge of each pillow back rectangle. Fold again, press, and sew to create a finished edge.

4. Turn the hemmed edges under 2″, wrong sides of the fabric together, and press.

5. Place the smaller pillow back rectangle on top of the completed pillow top, wrong sides together, and pin. Place the second pillow back rectangle on top of this unit and pin. The pillow back sections should overlap each other.

Baste around the edges of the pillow sections with a scant ¼″ seam. The area in the back where the pillow back sections overlap will allow you to insert the pillow form into the pillow.

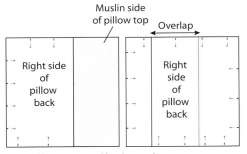

Pin and baste top and back together.

6. Bind the edges of the pillow. Insert the pillow form.

Social Circles Pillow

Karla Menaugh

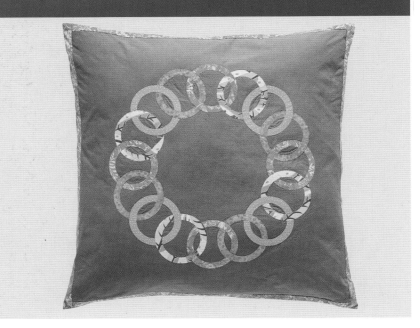

Social Circles *recalls Emporia's community of quiltmakers and the network of garden societies, quilting groups, churches, and bridge clubs that drew small-town women together in the 1930s. Although the geometries in the pattern look quite modern, the interlocked rings are found in several album quilts from the mid-nineteenth century!*

Materials and Cutting

Because the appliqué process tends to shrink the background slightly, the background piece is cut oversized. You will trim it to size after the appliqué is finished. Yardage is based on 42"-wide fabric.

Refer to the pillow photo to guide color placement.

Fabric	For	Cutting
2 yards dark gray solid	Background for front and back	1 square 24" × 24" 2 rectangles 14½" × 23"
½ yard blue print	Border for front and back	4 strips 1¼" × width of fabric; subcut a 23" strip and a 15¼" strip from each 2 strips 1¼" × 24½"
	Rings	See pattern (page 30); photocopy at 200% and cut 4 rings.
10" square each of yellow, orange, and lime-green print	Rings	See pattern (page 30); photocopy at 200% and cut 4 rings from each color.
24" pillow form		

KARLA MENAUGH is a journalist and editor with experience in both newspapers and public relations. With Barbara Brackman, she managed the Sunflower Pattern Cooperative, a successful quilt pattern company, for nearly ten years. Karla is skilled at machine quilting techniques, particularly machine appliqué, and teaches in guilds and shops. She lives near Louisville, Kentucky.

This project originally appeared in *Emporia Rose Appliqué Quilts* by Barbara Brackman and Karla Menaugh, available from C&T Publishing.

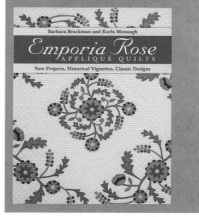

Construction

MAKING THE PILLOW TOP

1. Appliqué the rings onto the 24" background square. You will need to cut every other ring and hide the cut ends under the adjacent ring. Trim the square to 23" × 23", making sure the design is centered.

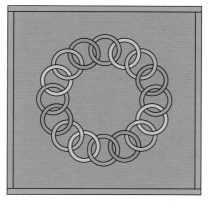

2. Sew a 23" blue strip to 2 opposite sides of the Social Circles block.

3. Sew a 24½" blue strip to the remaining sides of the block to complete the pillow front.

MAKING THE PILLOW BACK

1. Sew a 23" blue strip to a long side of each of the 14½" × 23" gray rectangles.

2. Sew a 15¼" blue strip to each short side of the rectangles from Step 1.

3. Turn under ¼" along the long gray side of each rectangle, and press. Fold again ¾" and press. Topstitch ⅛" from the inner folded edge of each to create a hem.

PILLOW ASSEMBLY

1. Place the pillow front faceup on a flat surface.

2. Place a pillow back rectangle facedown on top of the pillow front, lining up the blue borders on the back with the blue borders on one side of the front. Pin.

3. Place the remaining pillow back facedown on the other side of the pillow front, matching the blue borders with the pillow top. The rectangles will overlap in the center.

4. Stitch a ¼" seam around the outside edge of the pillow.

5. Trim the corners at a diagonal and turn the pillow right side out.

6. Insert the pillow form.

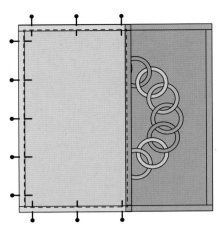

Berry Vine Pillow

Jessica Levitt

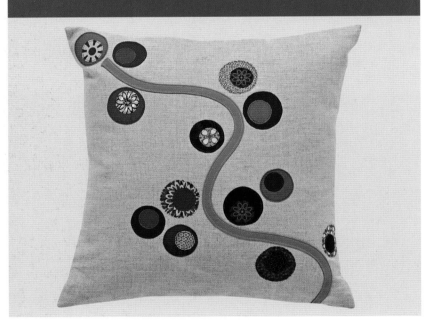

FINISHED PILLOW:
13½", 15½", or 17½" square

Beautiful textured linen makes a nice backdrop for some fun, modern "berries." The raw-edge appliqué makes this pillow a cinch to complete. I made it with a combination of prints and solids, but it would work equally well with all solid fabrics. Instructions and yardage are provided for three different sizes: 14″, 16″, and 18″ pillow forms.

tip For this project, you need a ½" bias tape maker. Of course, you can also buy premade fusible bias tape, but where's the fun in that?

Materials

LINEN/LINEN BLEND: ⅝ yard for 14" or 16" pillow; ¾ yard for 18" pillow (for front and back)

SOLID 1: 1 fat quarter for vine

SOLID SCRAPS: for berries

PRINT SCRAPS: for berries

PILLOW FORM:
14", 16", or 18" square*

FUSIBLE WEB:
1 sheet 9" × 12"

* The cover is sewn ½" smaller than the pillow form for a nice, firm pillow.

Cutting

14" PILLOW

Linen: Cut 1 square 14½" × 14½", 1 rectangle 11" × 14½", and 1 rectangle 8½" × 14½".

16" PILLOW

Linen: Cut 1 square 16½" × 16½", 1 rectangle 13" × 16½", and 1 rectangle 8½" × 16½".

18" PILLOW

Linen: Cut 1 square 18½" × 18½", 1 rectangle 15" × 18½", and 1 rectangle 8½" × 18½".

FOR ALL SIZES

Solid 1: Cut 1 bias strip 1" wide across the diagonal of the fabric.

Construction

All seams are ½″ unless otherwise noted.

PREPARE THE APPLIQUÉS

1. Trace the patterns (page 29) onto the fusible web to make 7 each of the 2″- and 1¼″-diameter circles, and 6 each of the 1¾″- and 1″-diameter circles. If preferred, use fewer appliqués on the smaller pillow or more on the larger one.

2. Cut loosely a little outside each circle. Peel off the unmarked side of the paper and stick it onto the wrong side of the solid and print scraps. Now cut precisely on the lines through all layers.

SEW THE VINE

1. Fold both long edges of the bias strip in ¼″ to meet in the center; press.

2. Lay your bias tape wrong side down onto the right side of the linen square (14½″, 16½″, or 18½″). Arrange the bias tape into a squiggle or any shape desired. The bottom end should extend off the edge of the square. Pin it in place with plenty of pins. To get the bias tape to lie flat, stretch the outside edge as you go around a curve. Cut the top end to the desired length, tuck it under ¼″, press, and pin.

3. Topstitch close to the edge along all sides of the bias tape, keeping the tape flat as you sew.

ADD THE BERRIES

1. Pair the circles, placing a 1¼″ circle on top of each 2″ circle and a 1″ circle on top of each 1¾″ circle. Peel the backing paper off the smaller circles and stick them in place on the larger circles so that they are off-center.

2. Peel the paper off the larger circles and stick them along the vine in a somewhat random manner. Use the photo as a guide if you desire. Add extra circles or remove some if desired. When you are pleased with the arrangement, fuse them in place according to the manufacturer's instructions.

3. Topstitch close to the edge all the way around each circle.

COMPLETE THE PILLOW

1. Press under ½″ along one long edge of each remaining linen rectangle. Tuck the raw edges into the fold and press again. Topstitch ⅛″ from the folded edge.

2. Lay the smaller hemmed rectangles on top of the larger one, right sides facing up, overlapping the hems to create a square the same size as the front (14½″, 16½″, or 18½″). Pin in place and baste along the sides ¼″ from the edges.

JESSICA LEVITT has been sewing and quilting since the age of 12. Always thirsting for some new craft, she has taught herself countless quilting techniques as well as costuming, event design, and home decor. She has also designed several lines of fabric for Windham Fabrics. Jessica lives and works in New Jersey.

WEBSITE: juicy-bits.typepad.com

This project originally appeared in *Modern Mix* by Jessica Levitt, available from Stash Books.

3. Pin the pillow front and back together, right sides together. Stitch around all 4 sides with a ½″ seam. Trim corners and turn right side out through the back opening.

4. Insert the pillow form through the opening in the back.

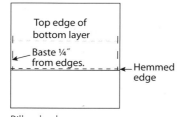

Pillow back

Patterns

Starflower Pillow

(page 3)

Starflower Pillow
Large petal

Starflower Pillow
Small petal

Hopscotch Pillow

(page 14)

Hopscotch Pillow
Small Circle

Row, Row Your Boat Patchwork Cushion Cover

(page 12)

More Tea? Pillow (page 6)

NOTE: The patterns do *not* include a ¼" (6 mm) seam allowance (except in places where a piece will be underneath another appliqué).

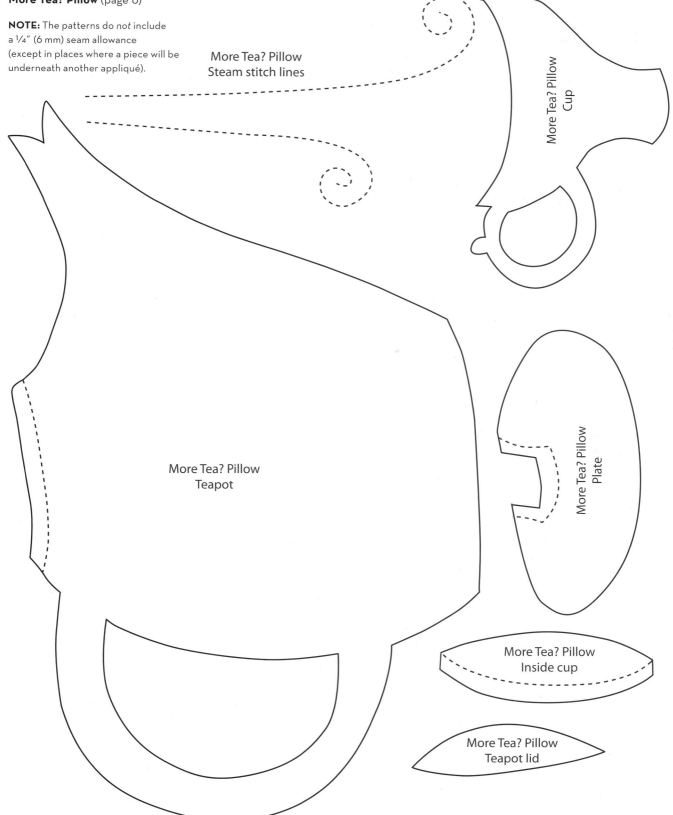

More Tea? Pillow
Steam stitch lines

More Tea? Pillow
Cup

More Tea? Pillow
Teapot

More Tea? Pillow
Plate

More Tea? Pillow
Inside cup

More Tea? Pillow
Teapot lid

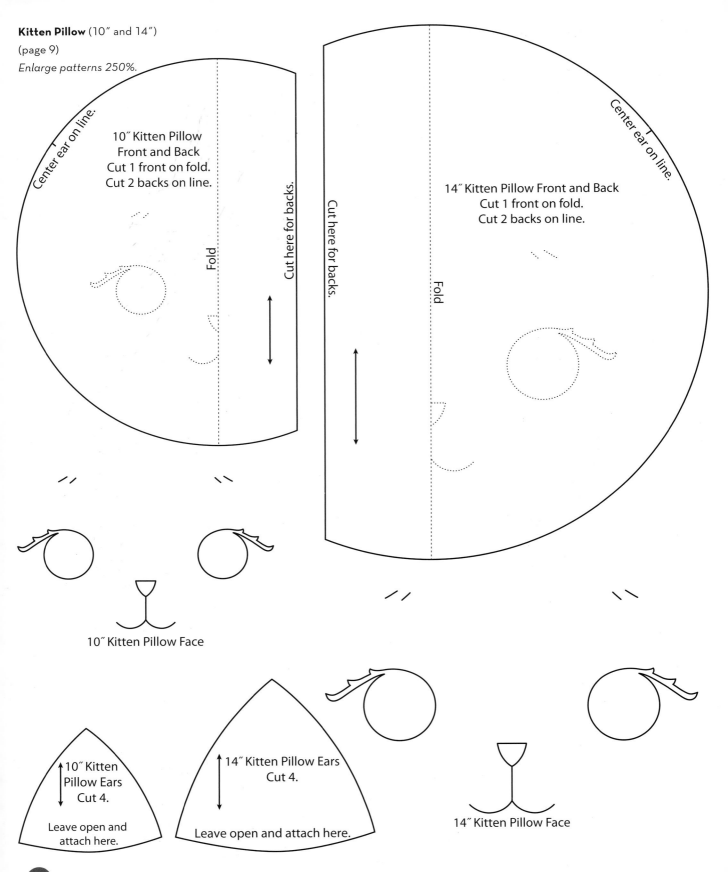

Kitten Pillow (10" and 14")

(page 9)

Enlarge patterns 250%.

Center ear on line.

10" Kitten Pillow
Front and Back
Cut 1 front on fold.
Cut 2 backs on line.

Fold

Cut here for backs.

Center ear on line.

Cut here for backs.

Fold

14" Kitten Pillow Front and Back
Cut 1 front on fold.
Cut 2 backs on line.

10" Kitten Pillow Face

10" Kitten
Pillow Ears
Cut 4.

Leave open and
attach here.

14" Kitten Pillow Ears
Cut 4.

Leave open and attach here.

14" Kitten Pillow Face

Blooming Season Pillow (page 11)

Berry Vine Pillow

(page 24)

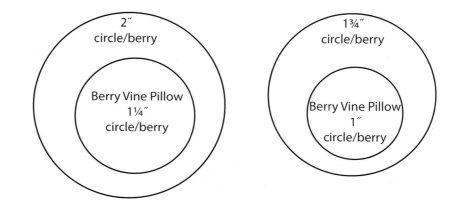

2″
circle/berry

Berry Vine Pillow
1¼″
circle/berry

1¾″
circle/berry

Berry Vine Pillow
1″
circle/berry

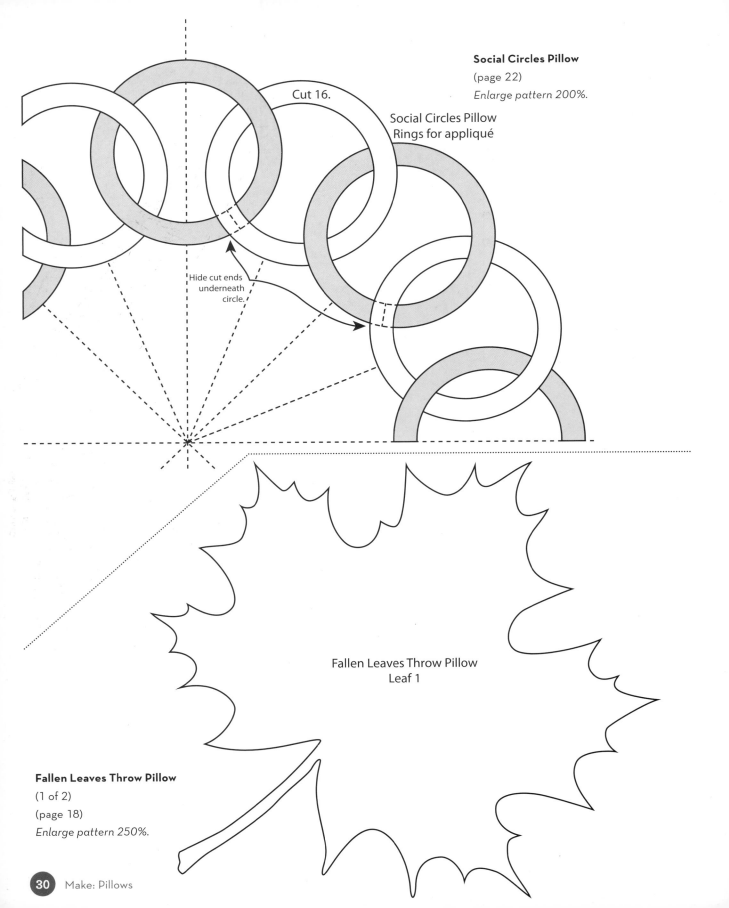

Social Circles Pillow
Social Circles Pillow
(page 22)
Enlarge pattern 200%.

Cut 16.

Social Circles Pillow
Rings for appliqué

Hide cut ends
underneath
circle.

Fallen Leaves Throw Pillow
Leaf 1

Fallen Leaves Throw Pillow
(1 of 2)
(page 18)
Enlarge pattern 250%.

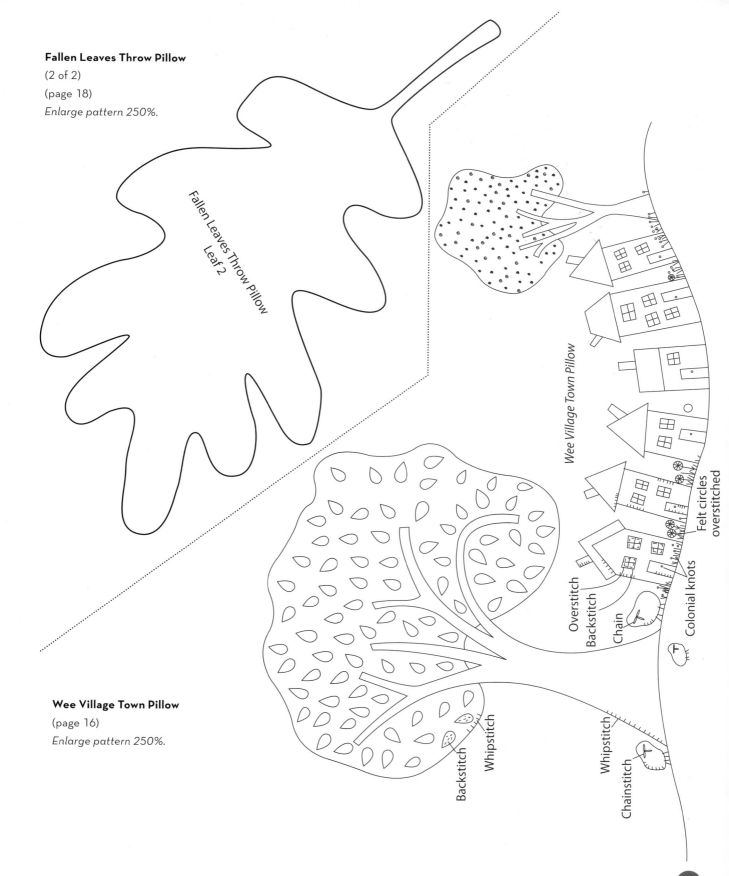

Fallen Leaves Throw Pillow

(2 of 2)

(page 18)

Enlarge pattern 250%.

Fallen Leaves Throw Pillow
Leaf 2

Wee Village Town Pillow

Felt circles
overstitched

Overstitch
Backstitch
Chain

Colonial knots

Wee Village Town Pillow

(page 16)

Enlarge pattern 250%.

Backstitch
Whipstitch

Whipstitch
Chainstitch

Breeze Pillow

(page 20)

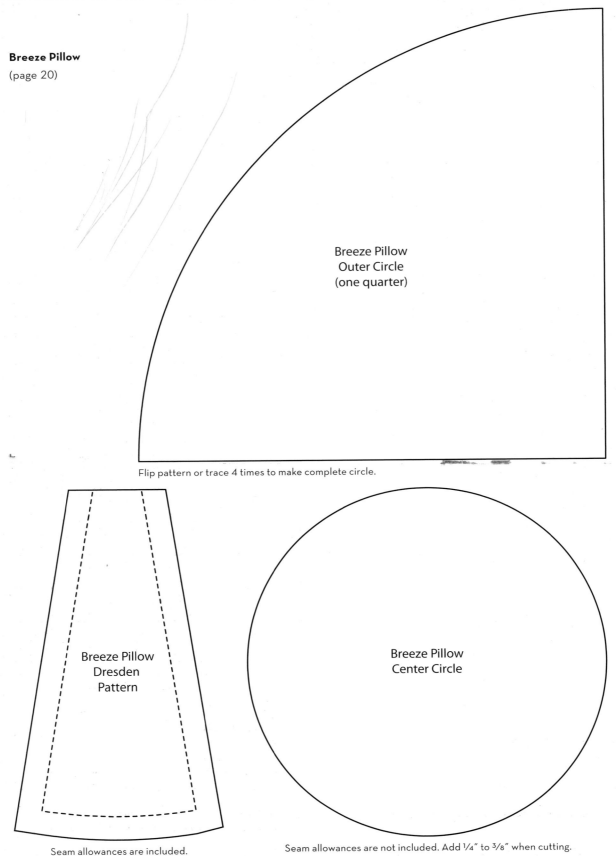

Breeze Pillow
Outer Circle
(one quarter)

Flip pattern or trace 4 times to make complete circle.

Breeze Pillow
Dresden
Pattern

Breeze Pillow
Center Circle

Seam allowances are included.

Seam allowances are not included. Add 1/4" to 3/8" when cutting.